Original title:
Purpose in the Pockets of Life

Copyright © 2025 Creative Arts Management OÜ
All rights reserved.

Author: Amelia Montgomery
ISBN HARDBACK: 978-1-80566-253-2
ISBN PAPERBACK: 978-1-80566-548-9

Echoes Between the Cracks

In the couch, a stray coin sings,
It jingles tales of forgotten things.
Lost socks plot their daring escape,
While crumbs scheme and make their shape.

The fridge hums a lullaby tune,
As leftovers tango under the moon.
A rogue pen rolls, but it's not alone,
With sticky notes forming a throne.

The Magic in the Mundane

The dust bunnies dance beneath my bed,
Each one fully-sized with clever dread.
The laundry basket's a mountain high,
Worn jeans whisper, 'Don't say goodbye!'

A spoon and fork stage a grand duel,
While dish soap bubbles play it cool.
In the kettle, tea leaves spin a tale,
As steam rises, they set sail.

Notes from the Quiet Corners

Untamed shoelaces form a crew,
Plotting pranks on feet that woo.
A cat nabs the sunbeam's warm glow,
While shadows play tag, moving slow.

The calendar yearns for a day-off,
As months bicker and then scoff.
In the closet, moths dance a jig,
While forgotten sweaters hug a fig.

Subtle Sparks of Connection

The bottom of the bag holds true gold,
Old receipts from tales once told.
A crumpled map lies, oh how it dreams,
Of adventures lost in forgotten streams.

The coffee mug gives sage advice,
Blending wisdom with a splash of spice.
A spoon's reflection shares a grin,
As everyday magic begins to spin.

Navigating through the Nooks

In cupboards deep, where socks go missing,
A treasure hunt turns to sock-puppy kissing.
We peek and we prod in the kitchen's maze,
  Finding leftovers from last month's craze.

  Behind the couch, a tangle of dust,
    Where crumbs together start to rust.
   I swear that I saw a lost remote,
And found an old sandwich, nice and afloat!

Discoveries in the Ordinary

In coffee cups, the secrets thrived,
As caffeine whispers 'you've survived!'
Each mug, a tale of morning feats,
With snickers shared, my life repeats.

Beneath the bed, a world of dust,
Where old shoes gather, it's a must.
I stumble on mismatched socks galore,
And ponder why I bought those before!

The Weight of a Whisper

A sneeze, a chuckle, it's loud as a bell,
When secrets spill, oh do tell!
We hush the room, with all our might,
But laughter leaks out, like shadows at night.

In corners, we stash our inside jokes,
Like silly hats on forgetful folks.
Whispered giggles float on air,
While dance moves erupt from the dining chair!

Heartbeats of Commitment

In laundry folds, our stories wait,
Each shirt a stanza, a twist of fate.
The dryer croons a love song warm,
While mismatched socks, they raise alarm.

Calendars filled with dates gone by,
Heart-shaped reminders, oh my, oh my!
We plan and plot, like quirky spies,
In the mundane, hope often lies!

The Color of Thought

In the garden of ideas, colors collide,
A blue thought giggles, while yellow swings wide.
Red whispers secrets with a green little wink,
As purple makes lemonade from what others think.

Orange jumps high, wearing mismatched socks,
While the pink clouds dance, playing with clocks.
Every hue has a story, a tickle or jest,
In this wild palette, it's a colorful quest.

Moments that Matter Most

Once I spilled coffee—what a great mess!
It splattered like art; oh, I must confess!
From chaos, I laughed, and the cat joined the fun,
Chasing the drips, till the chaos was done.

The microwave dinged, a burnt popcorn tale,
In the kitchen disaster, I stumbled and flailed.
Yet, laughter erupted, like a sudden bright song,
In these tiny moments, we find where we belong.

Mapping the Smallest Journeys

A pebble rolled away on a journey so grand,
It traveled to places where only ants stand.
It met a lost sock, once tossed in despair,
Now they plot their adventure without any care.

From couch to the fridge, they wander like fools,
Creating new paths that ignore all the rules.
There's magic in corners of dust bunnies' lands,
Each small little quest, it's all close at hand.

The Potency of Small Acts

I waved at a squirrel; he waved back with delight,
A high-five with feathers, what a silly sight!
I shared fries with strangers, what a tasty surprise,
Each moment we chirp makes the world more wise.

A fumble on the sidewalk turned into a dance,
We twirled and we laughed, giving life a chance.
These small silly snippets, so easy to miss,
Are treasures we gather, each giggle a bliss.

The Symphony of Small Triumphs

A sock that matches is a real big score,
Finding loose change? Who could ask for more?
The art of brewing that perfect cup,
A toast to success, let's all raise up!

The cat's on the counter, claiming the throne,
While the dog looks up as if he's been shown.
Silly little wins that make you feel bright,
In this crazy circus, we'll dance in the light.

Reflections in the Stillness of Routine

Waking up to the sound of a snooze,
Coffee's like magic, can't lose this muse.
The toast pops up, it's a thrilling ride,
Butter melting down, it's like a joy slide.

Walking the dog, who stops to greet,
A squirrel steals the spotlight, quite the feat.
Routine's a canvas where laughter can sprout,
Finding the humor in what life's about.

Life's Mosaic of Hidden Meanings

A sock puppet show with just one odd sock,
The mysteries of laundry, a strange paradox.
Crumbs on the sofa, a treasure trove,
I swear this snack route leads to a hidden grove!

A coffee spill marks where my day began,
Each little flub, a quirky, strange plan.
In life's wacky quilt, we stitch and we sew,
Finding bright patterns in a common show.

Glimmers of Hope in Ordinary Ruins

A plant that won't die, what a rare miracle,
And surviving a week on mere cereal.
The phone that won't die and keeps me informed,
The chaos of life; how it perfectly's formed!

My ice cream has melted, but here's the bright side,
A chocolate river, let's take a glide.
In the mess of our lives, we laugh and we cheer,
Finding small glimmers is the highlight here.

Whispered Aspirations

In the corner of my sock drawer,
A dream was tightly wedged,
I thought it was a sandwich,
Instead, it asked for wedged.

Old shoelaces, a tangled mess,
Whisper tales of bold adventures,
But my sneakers are shy and quiet,
Dreams dance when I don't venture.

A pencil with a missing lead,
Wants to write a novel, bright,
But first, it must be sharpened,
And find its muse tonight.

So I rummage through the clutter,
For gems hidden from view,
A ticket stub, an errant note,
All giggling, who knew?

The Light Within the Shadows

Once a shadow had a dream,
To be a spotlight on stage,
It stumbled on a banana peel,
Declaring, 'I'm the new age!'

Post-its dance on my windowsill,
Each color sings with glee,
'We have plans for world domination!'
'I just want my coffee!' cries the tea.

A stray sock with holes galore,
Decides it wants to fly,
But instead of takeoff,
It lands with a little sigh.

In the depths of every closet,
A mischief lurks awake,
Finding joy in the mundane,
All it needs is a cake!

Unraveling Cerulean Threads

In a world of tangled yarn,
A sweater dreams of grace,
But all it's making is a mess,
It can't find the right place.

A bluebird sings a jolly tune,
From the pocket of my coat,
But is quickly chased away,
By my worried, wild goat.

Glitter stuck upon the floor,
Sparks joy every time I trip,
It shimmers like a secret,
When I fall upon my hip.

So let's twirl in chaos sweet,
And find the fun inside,
Because life's an artful puzzle,
With laughter as our guide.

Picking Wildflowers Along the Way

A dandelion and I conspired,
To make a crown of gold,
But a bee buzzed in, all flustered,
'You're forgetting to be bold!'

Picking daisies, one by one,
I crafted a bouquet bright,
But tripped on a rogue garden hose,
'That's me, the queen of flight!'

The sunflowers looked down and laughed,
'Nice hat, made with glee!'
They swayed like they were in a band,
'Now come and dance with me!'

Now, I strut with petals proud,
And wear my wildflower crown,
For happiness grows in odd places,
Even when I fall down!

Maps of Discovery in Unmarked Trails

In the woods I found my way,
A squirrel stole my lunch today.
He winked as he ran off with glee,
Guess it was his pick-a-berry spree.

A compass spins, I try to steer,
But the trees just laugh—oh dear!
A bush told me to take a rest,
So now I'm lost—why? I'm the best!

My shoes are muddy, pants askew,
But hey, at least my socks are blue!
I've spotted critters having tea,
A picnic party just for me!

The path leads on, but do I care?
Here's a chipmunk, I need to share!
Maps that show the trails ahead,
Are nothing 'til you've lost your bread!

The Resonance of Unnoticed Joys

In a garden, weeds do dance,
I tripped and gave them all a chance.
They whispered secrets, oh so sly,
Like, "Who needs order? Just let it fly!"

A cup of tea, I spill with flair,
The cat just stares, gives me that glare.
But hey, a droplet's on his nose,
Now he's stuck in a soggy pose!

At the bus stop, life's a stage,
An old man shows off his new age.
With every story, laughter rolls,
As pigeons join in, stealing souls!

So, swing a smile at every wall,
Life's little joys partake in the brawl.
Let's twirl in circles, not ask why,
For happiness lurks where we defy!

Tapestries Woven with Threads of Life

My sweater's knitted, full of holes,
A work of art, or is it foals?
Each stitch to tell a tale of yore,
Of coffee spills and late-night snore.

The mismatched buttons gleam with pride,
Each one a secret I can't abide.
A friend says, "Fashion? You ignore!"
I wink, and twirl, who could ask for more?

In the kitchen, flour flies astray,
My cake's a pancake—who's to say?
Frosting drips with sugary cheer,
Call it abstract, my masterpiece here!

My tapestry's a crazy quilt,
With threads of joy and even guilt.
So grab a laugh from every plight,
And weave your days in pure delight!

Fables of Fulfillment in Daily Rituals

Each morning's quest, I brew my tea,
A dance with mugs, just wait and see.
I spill some love, add sarcasm too,
    A sip of joy, that'll surely do!

With toast in hand, I jam with flair,
My knife's a sword—quick! Beware!
    The butter slips, a slippery foe,
My breakfast dreams refuse to glow.

At work, my papers plot a coup,
    They fly away, a paper zoo!
A stapler stuck in a rebel's plight,
As post-its party, bright and light.

So laugh with me as we explore,
These daily tales we can't ignore.
For in each mishap, small or grand,
Lie fables that we've all planned!

Whispers of Intent

In the fridge, a pickle waits,
Briefly pondering its fates.
Should it garnish a grand feast,
Or hide as a tangy beast?

A sock lost in the dryer dance,
Hoping for a second chance.
Will it find a partner soon?
Or be a lone, striped buffoon?

A cat's slow blink, a secret plan,
To leap on the bed and be the man.
In a world so full of fluff,
Life's absurd, but that's enough!

Beneath the couch, crumbs conspire,
Plotting snacks they can acquire.
All these tidbits may seem small,
But they're the joy that bonds us all.

Threads of Meaning

The yarn rolls out with little care,
A kitten darts — a playful scare.
Each thread has dreams of scarves and hats,
But ends up tangled with goofy spats.

A single shoe left on the mat,
Wonders where its friend has sat.
Will it wander or stay put?
Life's oddities in a toe nail's rut.

An overripe banana, oh so sly,
Hopes for a smoothie, but it might die.
Yet in this fruit, a lesson grows,
Embrace the funk, who really knows?

The clock ticks loud, it might complain,
"Time is money," it screams in vain.
Yet in the chaos we might find,
Joy in moments, humor entwined.

Small Avenues of Significance

A spoon stands proud beside a knife,
Mocking forks while leading life.
With every scoop and every slice,
They craft the meal — oh, how nice!

Pigeons strut with regal airs,
Pecking crumbs without a care.
They plot their seeds of lunchtime bliss,
And point the way to urban hiss.

In a garden, weeds might thrive,
While daisies dance and feel alive.
But even those pesky green foes,
Offer shade where the sunlight flows.

A paperclip, so stoic, grand,
Holds together what's unplanned.
In chaos, it keeps life in line,
Little things can truly shine.

Hidden Gems of Existence

A taco shell, quite full of cheer,
Dreams of guac and beans near.
But life's a dance, and what a fuss,
Will it hold or make a mess of us?

Sweaters hug the winter chill,
One with holes, a fashion thrill.
It thinks it's vintage, oh so fine,
But really looks like it crossed the line.

Bubbles float and dance in air,
Each a wish, a puffy prayer.
But when they pop, what's left behind?
An echo of laughter, joy defined.

And in the garden, gnomes stand guard,
Their thoughts a mystery, but not too hard.
What purpose do they serve, you ask?
Perhaps just to be, a cheerful task!

Moments that Mold the Spirit

In the morning, socks don't match,
I laugh as I make a snatch.
Coffee spills, what a delight,
A caffeinated paper fight!

Chasing ducks at the park,
They quack back—quite the lark!
With bread crumbs, I'm a chef,
Dinner? Just a quack for the left!

Trip on a toy, down I go,
Laughter filters through the woe.
A cat's tail swipes the floor,
Suddenly, I'm not bored anymore!

On a rollercoaster ride, I scream,
Who knew fear could burst the seam?
Life's a carnival, full of glee,
With cotton candy and a bee!

Lighthouses Found in Simple Gestures

A wink from a stranger in the mall,
Spreads joy like a paper ball.
A sneeze brings laughter, what a sight,
Sharing tissues, feeling light!

Door held open with great flair,
A polite gesture, beyond compare.
Falling in puddles, splashing round,
The giggles echo, joy unbound.

Handwritten notes on the fridge,
Snacks in pockets like a bridge.
A wink from my dog, he's so sly,
His eyes sparkle with a "Oh my!"

An umbrella given, just in time,
Dancing in rain feels like a rhyme.
Laughter in chaos, smiles so bright,
Tiny lighthouses guide me right!

The Poetry Within the Everyday

A cereal box, a pirate's chest,
Treasure found, I am the best!
Milk rivers flow, a sugary sea,
On this journey, just me and me!

A napkin sketch of a dancing cat,
Creative juice spills like that!
Each bite of toast, a sunny tune,
Life's a banquet in afternoon.

In the laundry, socks hold hands,
Together they weave joyful plans.
Mismatched pairs, a comedy,
It's all about the irony!

Upon the couch a dance unfolds,
Remote in hand, a king of bolds.
Every click a magic spell,
Who knew such joy at home could dwell!

The Journey to Unveil the Unnoticed

On the road of little things,
Where mismatched socks find their fling,
I stumbled on a rubber duck,
Wearing shades, oh what a luck!

With a cupcake hat and a grin,
It gave a wink, told me to spin,
A traffic cone said, 'Don't be late,'
While dancing with a slice of fate!

Life's a treasure hunt, they say,
In grocery aisles, we'll find our way,
With every cart that bumps and sways,
We giggle through the shopping maze!

So grab your maps of silly sights,
Let's race the sun in cartoon flights,
For even socks can save the day,
When laughter leads the goofy play!

Smiles in the Details of Existence

There's magic in a cat's meow,
While sneaky ants take a bow,
The butter on my toast loves dance,
Each crumb holds a secret chance!

Sidewalk chalk, with colors bold,
Draws hopscotch dreams like tales untold,
Bouncing smiles from kids nearby,
While pigeons practice their own sky high!

A squirrel in shades has found its groove,
Chasing acorns, it's on the move,
With every hop, a giggle's caught,
In every nut, a lesson taught!

So let's embrace the quirky tricks,
In life's big bag of silly picks,
To cherish every tiny jest,
And find delight in our strange quest!

The Subtle Brushstrokes of Fate

In a world where socks are paired with zeal,
And buttered toast has secret appeal,
A t-shirt whispers, 'Wear me bold,'
As it guards the laughter that won't grow old.

Underneath the kitchen sink,
A sponge is plotting, don't you think?
While dishes dance the waltz of grime,
And socks engage in a laundry crime!

The toaster pops with cheerful pride,
While coffee beans have secrets to hide,
Each spilled drop tells a story grand,
Of chuckles shared, like grains of sand!

So, let's embrace the odd brigade,
In playful mischief, let's parade,
For every quirk is fate's sweet tease,
In time, these smiles are sure to please!

Reveries Found in Mundane Sights

In the hallway of forgotten dreams,
A shoelace stretches, or so it seems,
Dust bunnies laugh, holding hands,
While cheesy socks make silly plans!

Behind the curtain, a dust mote winks,
While spoons are having fun, it thinks,
As they plot to start a musical cheer,
Strumming with the dishwasher near!

Laundry baskets hold a fashion show,
T-shirts and pants in a colorful row,
Rubber bands join in the display,
Making outfits for a gala play!

So when you glance at the mundane scene,
Remember who's laughing, kind and keen,
For in each corner, a giggle hides,
In everyday life, joy abides!

Silhouettes of Intent in Fleeting Hours

In shadows cast by lunch hour hues,
A snack left untouched, what's a friend to choose?
The clock ticks loud, with a mischievous smile,
Egg salad whispers, 'Just stay for a while!'

The synergy's high over spilled soda streams,
As giggles erupt from half-baked daydreams.
We race for the bus, yet arrive in a mess,
Life's little detours, oh what a success!

Between hurried steps and misplaced shoes,
Laughter erupts at the silliest cues.
With each little stumble, we gather our pride,
In moments of chaos, the joys can't hide!

So here's to the laugh, the moment, the fluke,
In life's grand design, we're all just a kook.
Let's dance in the thought of what makes life bright,
With shadows as guides, we bask in the light!

The Art of Cherishing Small Things

A crumb falls down, oh what a delight,
The cat makes a leap, oh what a sight!
Each tiny treasure that life tends to throw,
Like mismatched socks in a bright flow of snow.

A rubber band slings across the room,
It lands on the cake, while we laugh at the doom.
Each sip of tea, a comedy show,
With thoughts on the table, our giggles flow!

Tiny adventures in spoons and in forks,
As dinner's a stage for two witty dorks.
The simple joys are the heart's finest bling,
In this small little world, we make our hearts sing!

So cherish the moments as they fly by,
Like bubbles that dance under a clear open sky.
With laughter as fuel and love as our strings,
Life's art is defined in the small, silly things!

Echoes of Wonder in Daily Whispers

Morning brings wonders, like toast in a haze,
Sidewalks are speaking in whimsical ways.
The spider spins tales on a shimmering thread,
While coffee chats gossip of dreams in our heads.

Each wrinkle of time laughs at plans we once made,
In the chaos of life, the silliness played.
With laundry throwing tantrums and socks doing flips,
We gather up giggles from everyday trips.

A puddle reflects all the clouds in disguise,
With splashes of joy, how the day often flies.
Watching our shadows, we laugh at the scene,
In echoes of wonder, let life be our queen!

So here's to the whispers of fun on the run,
To moments that sparkle and never are done.
In the symphony small, let our hearts dance and sway,
For life's daily whispers make magic each day!

Inspiration from the Cracks in the Pavement

In cracks on the sidewalk, ideas take flight,
With weeds that perform an exuberant rite.
Pavement whispers secrets of wild dreams gone bold,
As ants stage a play where the earth meets the old.

A pebble rolls by, like a wayward grain,
While squirrels plot mischief with absolute gain.
Their acorns a kingdom, their chatter a song,
In nature's mad circus, we all can belong.

Each crack tells a story, a twist and a laugh,
From splashes of color to nature's own craft.
Life bounces in rhythm, and so do we too,
Inspiration's found in the odd and the new.

So let's skip a stone over lives that we've known,
And dance on the pavement, wherever we roam.
In the smallest of treasures and cracks on the way,
There's humor aplenty in livin' each day!

Lanterns in the Fog

In a world that's often hazy,
I stumbled on a light so crazy.
It flickered and danced just like a mime,
Whispering to me, "You're right on time!"

With every step, I tripped on air,
Finding giggles hidden everywhere.
The moon was laughing, a big old tease,
Guiding my path like a clown with keys.

Fog swirled around with jokes untold,
Illuminated by the brave and bold.
Like a wobbly penguin on a steep hill,
Life throws curveballs, lean in for the thrill.

So lanterns glow and shadows flip,
Join in the dance, embrace the quip.
In misty realms, let humor ring,
In the fog of life, we find our spring!

Currents of Intentionality

There's a river flowing with a cheeky grin,
Each splash a chuckle, a delightful spin.
I floated by on a gummy bear,
While fish in bow ties played solitaire.

Waves of whimsy wash over my feet,
Like meeting a friend who can't find their seat.
Intentions paddle, so wobbly and wild,
In this aquatic adventure, I feel like a child.

A babbling brook sings silly tunes,
As turtles breakdance beneath the moons.
Every twist and turn makes me giggle,
Chasing ducks in a synchronized wiggle.

So here in the currents, we learn and play,
Intent on fun, come what may.
Life's a splash party, just dive right in,
Where laughter flows, that's where we begin!

The Art of Everyday Alchemy

In morning light, I brew a potion,
Of coffee, chaos, and wild emotion.
Stirring in laughter, a sprinkle of cheer,
Who knew chemistry could feel like a beer?

I turned my socks into a stylish hat,
While my cat conducted a symphony chat.
Every mundane task, a magic spell,
Transforming the bowl into a wishing well.

Diapers and dishes, a gilded routine,
With a touch of mischief, I'm the queen.
Cereal confetti on the kitchen floor,
I'm mixing joy even when it's a chore.

So let the mundane swirl and twirl,
In the art of life, let whimsy unfurl.
Each moment flips like a pancake kiss,
In the everyday, find the spark of bliss!

Treasures Beneath the Surface

Digging in dirt with a plastic spade,
What I found was a playful charade.
Shiny rocks and a bottle cap,
Hoarding treasures that make me clap!

The garden gnomes wink and they nod,
Cheering on my excavation squad.
Worms twirl in a dance, quite absurd,
Who knew earth could be this much fun, word?

Unearthing laughter 'neath the daily grind,
With treasures in pockets you're sure to find.
Each pebble tells stories, wild and grand,
Of adventures waiting just underhand.

So search through the soil, the leaves, the roots,
Unlock the joy in the simplest loot.
Life's little gems are more than they seem,
For beneath the surface, there's magic to dream!

Finding Value in the Mundane

In a pile of laundry, socks unite,
A rebel gang that loves to fight.
They vanish without a trace each day,
Deciding to vacation far away.

The dishes dance, a clattering tune,
While the fridge hums a lazy afternoon.
Spatulas gossip, they know the score,
Chopping onions like never before.

A pen rolls under the couch to hide,
With a lonely pencil, their giggling bride.
They pen love notes or grocery lists,
Yet somehow end up in misfit lists.

We search for gold in a tin can's shine,
Finding lost treasures, oh how divine!
A dusty old ball or a forgotten shoe,
Life's little quirks are the best things to do!

The Essence Beneath the Surface

In the fridge, a jar of spicy pickles,
Hold the secrets of culinary tickles.
They whisper tales of summer delights,
Yet sometimes end up in lonely fights.

A garden gnome keeps watch on the weeds,
With a crooked smile, he silently leads.
His ceramic heart beats a little slow,
Chasing rabbits that put on a show.

Underneath the bed, dust bunnies reside,
A fluffy army with nowhere to hide.
They throw wild parties with stray socks and dust,
Celebrating wins in the land of rust.

In coffee cups, we find our dreams,
As we sip on hopes and caffeinated creams.
Life may pour from a spilled mug's mess,
But laughter bubbles, we're feeling blessed!

A Tapestry of Everyday Wonders

A moth dances close to the ceiling light,
A brave little flyer in the dead of night.
While the cat stares up, full of disdain,
Plotting revenge, it's all in the game.

The laundry piles high, a fashion award,
Each sock a rebel, a fashion-forward hoard.
They stage a protest every Thursday eve,
Refusing to pair up, it's hard to believe.

The toaster pops, on tune it sings,
Offering toast and a few burnt flings.
It knows our hopes for breakfasty bliss,
Yet laughter erupts with every hit or miss.

The vacuum sweeps on a quest for crumbs,
Performing a dance, it rocks and hums.
With dust bunnies spinning in wild ado,
We'll take a bow for our cleaner crew!

Lighthouses in Daily Drudgery

In the morning rush, we misplace our shoes,
Chasing our pets, oh, such silly blues.
Coffee spills over, a caffeinated flood,
We wonder if we'll ever escape the thud.

The mailman arrives, with packages galore,
Yet it's bills that knock on our door.
We cheer when a postcard from Grandma sails,
Only to hide the reminders of tales.

At noon, the clock appears to taunt,
It's lunchtime and still, we haven't daunt.
Sandwiches stacked high, a tower of pride,
With each tiny bite, our dreams collide.

In the evening glow, we flop on the couch,
As pillows conspire, steal some vouch.
Netflix and snacks, the grand finale show,
Laughing through life's crazy highlight reel, go!

Renewal in the Routine

Each morning begins with the same old drill,
Coffee spills while I trip on a hill.
Spatula dances with a pancake's request,
I laugh at the chaos, it feels like a jest.

Sock puppets tell me to find some more zest,
To embrace each small moment is truly the best.
Spinning in circles, I'm part of the show,
Who knew that a mop could bring so much glow?

Dishes talk back, they're surprisingly wise,
Plates juggling secrets, with mischievous eyes.
The same old grind is a treasure in disguise,
Each hiccup and laugh—a new surprise.

So here's to the dance in the dull everyday,
Finding new rhythms in the mundane ballet.
With giggles and gaffes, I'll waltz down the lane,
Each laugh is a note in my grand little refrain.

Reclaiming Lost Dreams

In the attic, my dreams had a cozy retreat,
Old bikes and toys all stacked in a heap.
Cobbled together, those relics so grand,
I'd ride through the clouds on a bright purple hand.

A paper airplane still dares to soar,
Whispers of wishes from long years before.
I blow off the dust from a notebook I find,
With blank pages waiting, new ideas unwind.

Lost in the chaos, a treasure map shows,
The path of the quirks that only time knows.
Reclaiming what's hidden, I grab at my heart,
With laughter and giggles, I'm ready to start.

So let's raise a toast to the dreams that we've missed,
Each silly mishap becomes part of the list.
Rebuilding my joy with a sprinkle of glee,
Those whimsical moments are setting me free.

Tokens of the Human Experience

Stuck in a line for my morning brew,
A metaphorical journey, a grand rendezvous.
Chatting with strangers like we're old pals,
Over steaming cups, we trade hearty laughs.

Lost in a blink, my wallet's misplaced,
It's just a few dollars for a jolly good taste.
The barista just grins as she hands me my cup,
'Your joy's on the house, now drink up, don't pout!'

Each moment's a token, a chip from the game,
Collecting these giggles, no two are the same.
A cat on a leash, oh what a delight,
Or a dog in a tutu—that's pure comic flight.

We dance through the odd, the mundane we'll cheer,
With mishaps and laughter, oh life's full of cheer.
Embracing the quirks in our grand little show,
These tokens remind me, we're never alone.

Bridges of Understanding

Two neighbors, one lawn, a crazy garden fight,
They bicker and banter over the wrong type of light.
Yet when the storm hits, they venture outside,
With umbrellas like boats, they take quite a ride.

A barbecue invite—might bring strange delight,
With burnt offerings serving as culinary fright.
Grilled veggies do tango, sausages wail,
Each charred little bite is a laugh, not a fail.

Building new bridges with giggles anew,
In kitchen disasters, the friendship just grew.
Exchanging odd tales while tripping on shoes,
Life's funny little moments help us share our views.

So here's to connections, no matter the form,
In love and in laughter, we weather the storm.
Building those bridges, let quirks intertwine,
In the comedy chaos, our hearts align.

Notes in the Margin of Life

In the margins of my day,
I scribble down a joke or two.
Coffee spills and cake plants sway,
Life's a circus, who knew?

With sticky notes and bright highlighters,
I track my whims, they come and go.
Like stealthy ninjas, late night biters,
They steal my time, put on a show.

The socks that vanish, then reappear,
Like magic tricks we cannot see.
I laugh as I check my rear,
Did I just lose my sanity?

But still I'll dance, just twirl about,
In all this chaos, I find my rhyme.
With every note, I scream and shout,
Oh, laughter is the perfect crime!

Threads Woven in Stillness

In the quiet, I find my thread,
A piece of joy, a sassy phrase.
I knit my moments, there's no dread,
Laughter weaves through my clumsy ways.

Each stitch a giggle, a playful tease,
In every loop, a silly face.
I craft a blanket just to please,
A patchwork quilt of funny grace.

With threads of red and blues so bright,
I patch the holes where chaos grew.
A tug here, a pull there, what a sight,
Who knew yarn could make me spew?

So in the stillness, I find my muse,
A tapestry of quirks and mirth.
With every knot, I get to choose,
To laugh at all that life's worth!

Love Letters from the Everyday

Oh sweet mundane, my dear affair,
I pen you notes on napkins stained.
You surprise me with your cheeky flair,
To find you here, I'm quite entertained.

The way you trip me on the floor,
And how you hide my favorite shoes.
You wrap my world in laughter's roar,
Each moment's rich with silly views.

With muffin crumbs and toast askew,
I seal my letters with a grin.
Your playful antics keep me new,
A dance in every kitchen spin.

So here's to you, my everyday,
You fill my heart with joyful sings.
In all your quirks, I find my way,
Through love letters, life's sweet flings!

Echoes of Quiet Triumphs

In quiet rooms, my triumphs ring,
Like bubbles popping, laughter bursts.
I celebrate each tiny thing,
From socks matched up to snack-time firsts.

With quiet victories, I stand tall,
My cereal lands in the perfect bowl.
Every small win, I sweetly call,
A personal anthem for my soul.

The neighbors hear my laughter soar,
As I juggle tasks with glee and flair.
From fumbling steps to the front door,
Every misstep's a dance we share.

So let them echo, let them chime,
These moments shine like beacons bright.
In each small win, I make the time,
To find true joy in funny light!

Navigating the Unseen Pathways

In the attic of my mind, I roam,
Finding socks that lost their home.
There's wisdom in that tangled mess,
A nudge to wear my Sunday dress.

The cat's decision to sit just there,
In front of the TV, is quite the dare.
But in her stare, I see the truth,
Life's a joke, we're all uncouth.

Chasing shadows in the yard,
I thought I'd grown, but I'm still marred.
Each corner holds a laugh or two,
Like tripping over my own shoe.

With mismatched keys in hand I stand,
Unlocking doors to dreams unplanned.
In every stumble, giggle, or slip,
Life's a quirky little trip.

Flecks of Light in the Routine

The coffee pot sings a morning tune,
It spills out dreams with a spoon.
Each sip a riddle, a chuckle or two,
Why do I drink it when I'm already blue?

In my fridge lives a moldy cheese,
It's grown a family, if you please.
I named them all, they're quite the crew,
They've seen more than I ever do.

The laundry basket's a mountain high,
I swear it's plotting, oh my, oh my!
With every shirt, a tale unfolds,
Of adventures lost or secrets told.

The clock's hands run wild, tick-tock-ing away,
Like a game of hide and seek in the fray.
But amid the chaos, a laugh I find,
Life's a sitcom, one of a kind.

Seeds of Intention in Timeless Spaces

In the garden of my backyard dreams,
I planted hopes, or so it seems.
But weeds are dancing, taking the stage,
Making my life look like a cage.

The timer goes off, it's dinner time,
But my dish turned out like a crime.
Such culinary skills, a real delight,
Who knew that pasta could take flight?

A bubble in my bath, a wish I throw,
I hope it swirls fast, like my to-do flow.
But it just pops, with a silly splash,
And I laugh at mirrors in the flash.

In every moment, sameness can hide,
But winks of wonder are lurking inside.
So let's embrace this wacky ride,
With laughter and sprinkles, let joy abide!

Unraveling the Fabric of Daily Wonders

In the weave of my worn-out chair,
Lives a thousand thoughts, some quite rare.
The crumbs, they tell stories, every snack,
Of late-night musings and a little flak.

The traffic light winks as I wait,
Inviting me to contemplate fate.
A squirrel darts by, with flair and zest,
Chasing a dream, I ponder the jest.

My list of things to do today,
Has turned into a game of 'delay'.
Each scribble's a riddle, a task askew,
Like finding the right shoe to match my blue.

In the mundane, a spark can ignite,
A giggle, a memory, a sheer delight.
So let's pluck joy from what seems routine,
For 'normal' is just a wacky cuisine.

Shadows of Aspirations

I tripped on goals that danced around,
Like socks that vanish without a sound.
Dreams hid behind the sofa's back,
While ambition played an all-out prank.

I scribbled plans on napkin scraps,
With coffee stains and midnight naps.
Yet every time I set a sail,
My wind-up toy would always fail.

I found my vision in a shoe,
Where laces tangled like my view.
Misguided paths taught me to roam,
In the chaos, I felt at home.

Between the laughs and clumsy falls,
I tucked my dreams inside the walls.
Turns out, I'm a jester's heir,
With purpose lurking everywhere!

Chasing Fleeting Glimmers

I chased a star beneath my bed,
It whispered 'dream' but giggled instead.
I stumbled through the light of noon,
Tiptoeing on a cartoon balloon.

The glitter fell from skies of gray,
As I juggled wishes in a playful way.
Fleeting glimmers danced my way,
But vanished quick like yesterday.

I asked a cat, 'What's next?' She yawned,
With paws that twitched, she carried on.
So I took a ride on a rainbow's tail,
And tumbled down with a silly wail.

In laughter's reflects, my path unwinds,
A comical twist in silly finds.
Embracing mischief, I'll never tire,
Chasing glimmers through the quagmire!

Breadcrumbs of Insight

I dropped some crumbs to trace my way,
Only to find a bird's buffet.
With insights pecked and scattered wide,
I followed them like a wild ride.

Each nugget led to laughter's gate,
Where wisdom giggled and felt great.
I thought I knew where I would hide,
Till breadcrumbs turned and took a slide.

A pie on windowsills did glimmer,
Yet wisdom feasted, growing slimmer.
Chasing crumbs like a hungry fox,
I came across some mismatched socks.

I learned that life's a quirky game,
Where insights show up dressed the same.
Following paths both weird and bright,
I'll dance with crumbs in sheer delight!

Echoes of the Heart's Compass

My heart's a compass quite askew,
With whispers pointing oddly too.
It shouts directions in puns and glee,
Leading me to places like a bee.

I asked it where the treasure lies,
It joked of chocolate in blue skies.
With every turn, a laugh or two,
Clueless yet blissful, I'd follow through.

In maps of giggles, it led me near,
To party hats and icy beer.
It tickled fancies with each decree,
Echoes bouncing, "Come dance with me!"

So here I waltz with joy and glee,
Trusting whispers that never flee.
For every compass in life's toy box,
Points to laughter, with no paradox!

Veins of Significance

In the jar of mismatched socks,
There's a wisdom few unlocks.
A button lost, but oh so grand,
Each stitch holds truths we understand.

A spoon that's bent, a mug that's cracked,
In every flaw, a smile is packed.
Life's oddities, they take their stand,
Remind us joy was always planned.

The sandwich crusts that we discard,
Hold secrets, often left unmarred.
In every bite, a tasty plight,
Laughter waits with every bite.

So treasure all your little finds,
For they are more than just designs.
Each quirk contains a tale or song,
In the chaos, we all belong.

Flecks of Light in the Shadow

In the fridge, a lone cucumber,
Sits and dreams of sunny slumber.
A forgotten snack, it shines so bright,
Dancing under the fridge's light.

The old alarm that never chimes,
Still holds the echoes of good times.
With every tick, a quirky spark,
Life's laughter hides in every dark.

A paperclip with a broken twist,
Once held together what we missed.
Now it flails in fun's embrace,
Reminding us to slow our pace.

So toast the trinkets, small yet grand,
That shape our lives, like silver sand.
In silly things, we find our cheer,
And that's the light we hold most dear.

Memories Hidden in the Fold

In the pockets of a faded coat,
Rest tales of laughter, like a boat.
A ticket stub, a smiley face,
Reminding us of that sweet place.

Crumbs of cookies from last week's bake,
Hide stories of how much we shake.
Each fold and crease, a laugh or tear,
In fabric lives a love affair.

A note that's crumpled, but so sweet,
Holds words of love, a little treat.
Unfold it gently, take a peek,
In simple things, we often speak.

So gather all the bits and bobs,
The silly quirks, the little flobs.
For in our folds, the memories gleam,
And life becomes a funny dream.

Threads of Connection

A shoelace tangled, oh what fun,
Each knot a dance, a silly run.
The tripping feet laugh through the air,
As life reminds us to beware.

The frayed edge of an old postcard,
Tells stories of adventures hard.
Funny faces in every light,
Memories shared in sheer delight.

The quirky mugs upon the shelf,
Each with a tale of its own self.
Sipping tea as laughter swirls,
Life's threads weave joy in zigzag pearls.

So look around, find joy's embrace,
In every twist, a happy face.
Connect the threads, let laughter flow,
For in the chaos, spirits glow.

Hidden Gems of Existence

In pockets deep, we hide our snacks,
A crumpled note, or laughter's tracks.
The gum wrapper holds tales of glee,
While pennies wish for a cup of tea.

Lost keys dance like a lightweight clown,
Falling down, but never a frown.
A missing sock, where could it be?
Maybe off on a trip with the TV.

Spilled coffee tells stories of need,
While toast tries its best not to plead.
In crumbs of life, we find our cheer,
Tiny treasures that draw us near.

So let's dig deep through life's oddities,
Finding joy in lost documentaries.
Each trinket, a laugh; each gaffe, a gem,
In this wacky world, we celebrate them!

Threads of Significance in Common Threads

In seams of laughter, we find our way,
A thread unwinds from socks on display.
Doodles in margins of notes we take,
Patches of chaos, the best kind of wake.

With every pull, another short tale,
Scarves of memories, if we dare to unveil.
Safety pins like superheroes stand,
Holding together our life's messy brand.

With every button that pops and rolls,
A giggle escapes, that fulfills our roles.
Often we slip on the banana peel,
Yet laughter threads love, that's the deal!

In fabric of moments, the glitter we weave,
Simple hilarious joys we must believe.
Every stitch telling secrets of fun,
Threads of existence, together we run!

The Heartbeat of Ordinary Moments

Tick-tock says the clock, a comical beat,
As shoes find the dance floor, a wobbly feat.
The toast pops up with a jaunty flair,
Cheerful breadcrumbs flying through the air!

Garden gnomes gossip, their secrets so sly,
While ants host meetings under the pie.
In the hum of a fridge, there's life quite loud,
Each buzz a reminder, of a life so proud.

Bathroom mirrors reflect silly poses,
The toothy grins, like funny roses.
In the shuffle of papers, we find a lost draw,
Tales of spatulas and laughs that don't withdraw.

So let's cherish the odd, embrace the gray,
For laughter dangles in the ordinary play.
In simple moments, we find our zest,
The heartbeat of life, a laugh at its best!

Lanterns in the Shadows of the Day

Under the bed, dust bunnies reside,
But they throw wild parties when no one's inside.
Lanterns flicker with giggles untold,
As chores transform into quests, brave and bold.

Morning coffee spills, like a comic's fall,
Turning sober moments into a free-for-all.
The cat walks the line of strict aristocracy,
As dogs hum a tune of pure ecstasy.

In attic corners, forgotten toys play,
Hosting wild gatherings at the end of the day.
A sippy cup's laugh echoes through time,
While bedtime becomes a heartfelt mime.

So let's shine bright in the laughter's away,
Embracing shadows turned into ballet.
Each chuckle a lantern lighting the way,
In life's wacky mix, let's dance, come what may!

Unearthing Simple Truths

In the drawer, a sock does stray,
Could it have thoughts, in its own way?
A mismatched dream, it tries to find,
A partner lost, but still quite kind.

Under the couch, a crumb does hide,
A feast for ants, oh what a ride!
They dance around, with glee in sight,
While I just search for lunch, what a plight!

Behind the curtain, dust bunnies scheme,
Plotting world takeovers, or so it seems.
Their fluffy fur, a curious sight,
Could they be couch kings, in the twilight?

The laundry basket sings its song,
It calls to me, "You've waited long!"
Yet every shirt has a story tall,
Of coffee spills and sticky wall.

The Seedlings of Aspirations

In the garden, weeds wear hats,
Pretending they're dignified, like aristocrats.
They look so fancy, they think they're grand,
But it's the flowers with the master plan!

A tomato plant dreams of being red,
While carrots whisper, "We're better in bread!"
Each leaf a giggle, in nature's game,
As veggies plot to change their fame.

The zucchini wishes it could be a star,
With glitter and glam, perhaps from afar.
But squash is a humble, modest sort,
Wants accolades, but seeks no court!

As raindrops fall, they laugh and play,
In the puddles, they all wish to stay.
Growing together, with sun and moon,
In the garden of wishes, they sing a tune.

Fleeting Moments' Riches

Time flies by on a paper plane,
It loops and twirls, free from the mundane.
Stamping its passport, it chases the fun,
While I sit here wishing I'd done what's begun.

Coffee spills on important sheets,
A caffeinated mess, where chaos meets.
Yet to me, it's just a morning's joke,
As I dash to wipe it, I'm bound to choke!

A goldfish dreams of grander seas,
While nibbling flakes like gourmet cheese.
In its bowl, it swims round and round,
In a world so vast, but where it's bound!

A cat naps soundly on my phone,
While I beg it to let me own,
Each purr a promise, of dreams in tune,
Lost in the whimsy, like a soft afternoon.

Echoes of Life's Ambitions

The fridge hums secrets of midnight snacks,
Its light shines bright, as hunger attacks.
Leftovers plan a theatrical night,
While I contemplate what to munch, it's quite a sight!

A broom twirls like a dancer with flair,
Chasing dust bunnies, jumping through air.
Each swish and sweep, a rhythm of grace,
In the battle of floors, it takes first place!

The microwave beeps, it's time to reheat,
In a rave of leftovers, it can't be beat.
Popcorn whispers, "Let's bounce and pop!"
While I just hope this meal won't flop!

Life's little antics, lost in the grind,
Moments like these, are treasures to find.
With laughter echoing through my abode,
In the chaos of life, these treasures explode!

Adventures in the Minimal

In a world of crumbs and odd socks,
I search for treasure in flimsy boxes.
With each lost penny, I do a dance,
Who knew the mundane could lead to chance?

A spoon for a sword, a cap for a crown,
I ride my cat like he won the town.
With a mishmash plan and a cup of tea,
Every day's a quest—come join me, please!

Grace Notes of Existence

With cereal spilled on a top hat's brim,
I ponder life while the fish swim.
In mismatched shoes and a polka-dot tie,
I chase a balloon, oh me, oh my!

I juggle oranges, oh look—they fly!
The cat thinks he's king, he's quite the sly.
Each clumsy waltz makes the neighbors smile,
We celebrate chaos, oh what a style!

The Canvas of Ordinary Dreams

With crayons and toast, I paint my fate,
On the backs of napkins—oh, isn't it great?
A splash of jelly, a smear of jam,
My masterpiece drips; I call it 'Spam'.

Each boring Tuesday is a canvas bright,
When laundry speaks wisdom, it feels just right.
I spin in circles till I get dizzy,
Complaining is fun—oh, it's so busy!

Footprints in the Sand of Time

While walking on beaches with flip-flops tight,
I make silly shapes, oh what a sight!
Each grain of sand tells a tale so grand,
Especially the ones stuck to my hand.

The waves laugh back, they tickle my toes,
I chase after seagulls—oh how it goes!
And with every splash, I shed my woe,
Life's a goofy dance, come join the show!

www.ingramcontent.com/pod-product-compliance
Lightning Source LLC
Chambersburg PA
CBHW071822160426
43209CB00003B/166